WEEKLY PRAYER JOURNAL

WRITTEN & DESIGNED BY SHALANA FRISBY

COPYRIGHT 2018. ALL RIGHTS RESERVED.
WWW.123JOURNALIT.COM

More information at: www.123journalit.com

First Printing: 2018
1 2 3 Journal It Publishing

Pocketbook 6x9-in. Format Size
Weekly Prayer Journal Series

THIS JOURNAL
BELONGS TO

MY PRAYER NOTES FOR THE WEEK OF _____ TO _____

MONDAY:

TUESDAY:

WEDNESDAY:

THURSDAY:

FRIDAY:

SATURDAY:

SUNDAY:

ANSWERED PRAYERS & THINGS I'M THANKFUL FOR THIS WEEK:

MONDAY:

TUESDAY:

WEDNESDAY:

THURSDAY:

FRIDAY:

SATURDAY:

SUNDAY:

ANSWERED PRAYERS & THINGS I'M THANKFUL FOR THIS WEEK:

MONDAY:

TUESDAY:

WEDNESDAY:

THURSDAY:

FRIDAY:

SATURDAY:

SUNDAY:

ANSWERED PRAYERS & THINGS I'M THANKFUL FOR THIS WEEK:

MONDAY:

TUESDAY:

WEDNESDAY:

THURSDAY:

FRIDAY:

SATURDAY:

SUNDAY:

ANSWERED PRAYERS & THINGS I'M THANKFUL FOR THIS WEEK:

MONDAY:

TUESDAY:

WEDNESDAY:

THURSDAY:

FRIDAY:

SATURDAY:

SUNDAY:

ANSWERED PRAYERS & THINGS I'M THANKFUL FOR THIS WEEK:

MY PRAYER NOTES FOR THE WEEK OF _______ TO _______

MONDAY:

TUESDAY:

WEDNESDAY:

THURSDAY:

FRIDAY:

- -
- -
- -
- -

SATURDAY:

- -
- -
- -
- -

SUNDAY:

- -
- -
- -
- -

ANSWERED PRAYERS & THINGS I'M THANKFUL FOR THIS WEEK:

MONDAY:

TUESDAY:

WEDNESDAY:

THURSDAY:

FRIDAY:

- -
- -
- -
- -

SATURDAY:

- -
- -
- -
- -

SUNDAY:

- -
- -
- -
- -

ANSWERED PRAYERS & THINGS I'M THANKFUL FOR THIS WEEK:

MONDAY:

TUESDAY:

WEDNESDAY:

THURSDAY:

FRIDAY:

SATURDAY:

SUNDAY:

ANSWERED PRAYERS & THINGS I'M THANKFUL FOR THIS WEEK:

MONDAY:

TUESDAY:

WEDNESDAY:

THURSDAY:

FRIDAY:

SATURDAY:

SUNDAY:

ANSWERED PRAYERS & THINGS I'M THANKFUL FOR THIS WEEK:

MY PRAYER NOTES FOR THE WEEK OF _______ TO _______

MONDAY:

TUESDAY:

WEDNESDAY:

THURSDAY:

FRIDAY:

SATURDAY:

SUNDAY:

ANSWERED PRAYERS & THINGS I'M THANKFUL FOR THIS WEEK:

MONDAY:

TUESDAY:

WEDNESDAY:

THURSDAY:

FRIDAY:

SATURDAY:

SUNDAY:

ANSWERED PRAYERS & THINGS I'M THANKFUL FOR THIS WEEK:

MONDAY:

TUESDAY:

WEDNESDAY:

THURSDAY:

FRIDAY:

SATURDAY:

SUNDAY:

ANSWERED PRAYERS & THINGS I'M THANKFUL FOR THIS WEEK:

MONDAY:

TUESDAY:

WEDNESDAY:

THURSDAY:

FRIDAY:

SATURDAY:

SUNDAY:

ANSWERED PRAYERS & THINGS I'M THANKFUL FOR THIS WEEK:

MONDAY:

TUESDAY:

WEDNESDAY:

THURSDAY:

FRIDAY:

SATURDAY:

SUNDAY:

ANSWERED PRAYERS & THINGS I'M THANKFUL FOR THIS WEEK:

MY PRAYER NOTES FOR THE WEEK OF _____ TO _____

MONDAY:

TUESDAY:

WEDNESDAY:

THURSDAY:

FRIDAY:

SATURDAY:

SUNDAY:

ANSWERED PRAYERS & THINGS I'M THANKFUL FOR THIS WEEK:

MONDAY:

TUESDAY:

WEDNESDAY:

THURSDAY:

FRIDAY:

SATURDAY:

SUNDAY:

ANSWERED PRAYERS & THINGS I'M THANKFUL FOR THIS WEEK:

MONDAY:

TUESDAY:

WEDNESDAY:

THURSDAY:

FRIDAY:

SATURDAY:

SUNDAY:

ANSWERED PRAYERS & THINGS I'M THANKFUL FOR THIS WEEK:

MONDAY:

TUESDAY:

WEDNESDAY:

THURSDAY:

FRIDAY:

SATURDAY:

SUNDAY:

ANSWERED PRAYERS & THINGS I'M THANKFUL FOR THIS WEEK:

MY PRAYER NOTES FOR THE WEEK OF _______ TO _______

MONDAY:

TUESDAY:

WEDNESDAY:

THURSDAY:

FRIDAY:

SATURDAY:

SUNDAY:

ANSWERED PRAYERS & THINGS I'M THANKFUL FOR THIS WEEK:

MONDAY:

TUESDAY:

WEDNESDAY:

THURSDAY:

FRIDAY:

SATURDAY:

SUNDAY:

ANSWERED PRAYERS & THINGS I'M THANKFUL FOR THIS WEEK:

MONDAY:

TUESDAY:

WEDNESDAY:

THURSDAY:

FRIDAY:

SATURDAY:

SUNDAY:

ANSWERED PRAYERS & THINGS I'M THANKFUL FOR THIS WEEK:

MONDAY:

TUESDAY:

WEDNESDAY:

THURSDAY:

FRIDAY:

SATURDAY:

SUNDAY:

ANSWERED PRAYERS & THINGS I'M THANKFUL FOR THIS WEEK:

MY PRAYER NOTES FOR THE WEEK OF _____ TO _____

MONDAY:

TUESDAY:

WEDNESDAY:

THURSDAY:

FRIDAY:

SATURDAY:

SUNDAY:

ANSWERED PRAYERS & THINGS I'M THANKFUL FOR THIS WEEK:

MONDAY:

TUESDAY:

WEDNESDAY:

THURSDAY:

FRIDAY:

SATURDAY:

SUNDAY:

ANSWERED PRAYERS & THINGS I'M THANKFUL FOR THIS WEEK:

MY PRAYER NOTES FOR THE WEEK OF _______ TO _______

MONDAY:

TUESDAY:

WEDNESDAY:

THURSDAY:

FRIDAY:

SATURDAY:

SUNDAY:

ANSWERED PRAYERS & THINGS I'M THANKFUL FOR THIS WEEK:

MONDAY:

TUESDAY:

WEDNESDAY:

THURSDAY:

FRIDAY:

SATURDAY:

SUNDAY:

ANSWERED PRAYERS & THINGS I'M THANKFUL FOR THIS WEEK:

MY PRAYER NOTES FOR THE WEEK OF _______ TO _______

MONDAY:

TUESDAY:

WEDNESDAY:

THURSDAY:

FRIDAY:

SATURDAY:

SUNDAY:

ANSWERED PRAYERS & THINGS I'M THANKFUL FOR THIS WEEK:

MONDAY:

TUESDAY:

WEDNESDAY:

THURSDAY:

FRIDAY:

SATURDAY:

SUNDAY:

ANSWERED PRAYERS & THINGS I'M THANKFUL FOR THIS WEEK:

MONDAY:

TUESDAY:

WEDNESDAY:

THURSDAY:

FRIDAY:

SATURDAY:

SUNDAY:

ANSWERED PRAYERS & THINGS I'M THANKFUL FOR THIS WEEK:

MONDAY:

TUESDAY:

WEDNESDAY:

THURSDAY:

FRIDAY:

SATURDAY:

SUNDAY:

ANSWERED PRAYERS & THINGS I'M THANKFUL FOR THIS WEEK:

MY PRAYER NOTES FOR THE WEEK OF ______ TO ______

MONDAY:

TUESDAY:

WEDNESDAY:

THURSDAY:

FRIDAY:

SATURDAY:

SUNDAY:

ANSWERED PRAYERS & THINGS I'M THANKFUL FOR THIS WEEK:

MONDAY:

TUESDAY:

WEDNESDAY:

THURSDAY:

FRIDAY:

SATURDAY:

SUNDAY:

ANSWERED PRAYERS & THINGS I'M THANKFUL FOR THIS WEEK:

MONDAY:

TUESDAY:

WEDNESDAY:

THURSDAY:

FRIDAY:

SATURDAY:

SUNDAY:

ANSWERED PRAYERS & THINGS I'M THANKFUL FOR THIS WEEK:

MONDAY:

TUESDAY:

WEDNESDAY:

THURSDAY:

FRIDAY:

SATURDAY:

SUNDAY:

ANSWERED PRAYERS & THINGS I'M THANKFUL FOR THIS WEEK:

MY PRAYER NOTES FOR THE WEEK OF _____ TO _____

MONDAY:

TUESDAY:

WEDNESDAY:

THURSDAY:

FRIDAY:

SATURDAY:

SUNDAY:

ANSWERED PRAYERS & THINGS I'M THANKFUL FOR THIS WEEK:

MONDAY:

TUESDAY:

WEDNESDAY:

THURSDAY:

FRIDAY:

SATURDAY:

SUNDAY:

ANSWERED PRAYERS & THINGS I'M THANKFUL FOR THIS WEEK:

MONDAY:

TUESDAY:

WEDNESDAY:

THURSDAY:

FRIDAY:

SATURDAY:

SUNDAY:

ANSWERED PRAYERS & THINGS I'M THANKFUL FOR THIS WEEK:

MONDAY:

TUESDAY:

WEDNESDAY:

THURSDAY:

FRIDAY:

SATURDAY:

SUNDAY:

ANSWERED PRAYERS & THINGS I'M THANKFUL FOR THIS WEEK:

MONDAY:

TUESDAY:

WEDNESDAY:

THURSDAY:

FRIDAY:

SATURDAY:

SUNDAY:

ANSWERED PRAYERS & THINGS I'M THANKFUL FOR THIS WEEK:

MONDAY:

TUESDAY:

WEDNESDAY:

THURSDAY:

FRIDAY:

SATURDAY:

SUNDAY:

ANSWERED PRAYERS & THINGS I'M THANKFUL FOR THIS WEEK:

MONDAY:

TUESDAY:

WEDNESDAY:

THURSDAY:

FRIDAY:

SATURDAY:

SUNDAY:

ANSWERED PRAYERS & THINGS I'M THANKFUL FOR THIS WEEK:

MY PRAYER NOTES FOR THE WEEK OF _____ TO _____

MONDAY:

TUESDAY:

WEDNESDAY:

THURSDAY:

FRIDAY:

SATURDAY:

SUNDAY:

ANSWERED PRAYERS & THINGS I'M THANKFUL FOR THIS WEEK:

MONDAY:

TUESDAY:

WEDNESDAY:

THURSDAY:

FRIDAY:

SATURDAY:

SUNDAY:

ANSWERED PRAYERS & THINGS I'M THANKFUL FOR THIS WEEK:

MONDAY:

TUESDAY:

WEDNESDAY:

THURSDAY:

FRIDAY:

SATURDAY:

SUNDAY:

ANSWERED PRAYERS & THINGS I'M THANKFUL FOR THIS WEEK:

MY PRAYER NOTES FOR THE WEEK OF _____ TO _____

MONDAY:

TUESDAY:

WEDNESDAY:

THURSDAY:

FRIDAY:

SATURDAY:

SUNDAY:

ANSWERED PRAYERS & THINGS I'M THANKFUL FOR THIS WEEK:

MY PRAYER NOTES FOR THE WEEK OF _____ TO _____

MONDAY:

TUESDAY:

WEDNESDAY:

THURSDAY:

FRIDAY:

SATURDAY:

SUNDAY:

ANSWERED PRAYERS & THINGS I'M THANKFUL FOR THIS WEEK:

____

____

____

____

____

MONDAY:

TUESDAY:

WEDNESDAY:

THURSDAY:

FRIDAY:

SATURDAY:

SUNDAY:

ANSWERED PRAYERS & THINGS I'M THANKFUL FOR THIS WEEK:

FRIDAY:

SATURDAY:

SUNDAY:

ANSWERED PRAYERS & THINGS I'M THANKFUL FOR THIS WEEK:

____

____

____

____

____

____

MONDAY:

TUESDAY:

WEDNESDAY:

THURSDAY:

FRIDAY:

SATURDAY:

SUNDAY:

ANSWERED PRAYERS & THINGS I'M THANKFUL FOR THIS WEEK:

MONDAY:

TUESDAY:

WEDNESDAY:

THURSDAY:

FRIDAY:

SATURDAY:

SUNDAY:

ANSWERED PRAYERS & THINGS I'M THANKFUL FOR THIS WEEK:

____

____

____

____

____

____

MONDAY:

TUESDAY:

WEDNESDAY:

THURSDAY:

FRIDAY:

SATURDAY:

SUNDAY:

ANSWERED PRAYERS & THINGS I'M THANKFUL FOR THIS WEEK:

MONDAY:

TUESDAY:

WEDNESDAY:

THURSDAY:

FRIDAY:

SATURDAY:

SUNDAY:

ANSWERED PRAYERS & THINGS I'M THANKFUL FOR THIS WEEK: